THE POET'S WORKBOOK

THE POET'S WORKBOOK

ten projects for creating new poems

Alison Chisholm

First published in 2012
by Caleta Publishing

Copyright © Alison Chisholm 2012

The moral right of the author has been asserted.

This book is sold subject to the condition that no part of it shall be reproduced, stored in a retrieval system (other than for the purposes of review), or transmitted in any form or by any means, electronic, mechanical, photocopying, recording or otherwise, without the prior permission in writing of the copyright owner.

ISBN   978-1-4716-1997-7

Printed and bound by Lulu.com

THE POET'S WORKBOOK

This hands-on guide will direct you through projects designed to help you create ten new poems while enhancing your writing skills.

Simply work at your own pace, beginning with the pre-writing stage and producing each first draft within the book. The embryo material is then left to 'settle' before redrafting and revision. Staying close to the project specifications will give you a poem; exploring around them will enrich the poem and make it more individual.

There's a blank page at the end of each project for you to write a finished version. Keep the workbook to remind yourself of the journey it took.

You will find plenty of hints and tips in the projects, and suggestions for the all-important refining and finishing. All these tips can be adapted and applied to any other projects. At the end of the book is a list of ideas allied to the ones you have already developed, then a further set of ideas for your next ten poems.

Happy writing!

PROJECT ONE

Three line stanzas - tercets - are built up to re-create a memory with plenty of imagery to animate the situation. We'll concentrate on free verse, but of course any rhyme pattern could be used, as long as the same pattern is applied throughout the poem.

PRE-WRITING

First, identify the memory on which you will focus. It could be taken from any time, but we'll engage with some event from your second decade, when you were entering and experiencing the teen years. It should be a single event rather than an ongoing occurrence. For example, the first day at a new school would be more evocative than schooldays in general.

Start with a list of special events that have some emotional significance for you, including both positive and negative situations. The first two possible ideas are offered, then there's space for you to add your own:

- First date
- Death of a family member/friend

When you've completed the list, without writing anything down take a moment to think about one event at a time. Begin with the overview. How clear are your recollections? What did you feel about the event when it happened? How has it affected you since? How do you feel about it now?

If there's a sense of joy or unease accompanying a memory, you have identified the one to use. If not, take yourself away from the list physically, and do something different to allow yourself to stop thinking about possible themes. Take at least half an hour, then come back to the list and you will probably find you are drawn to one event more than the rest. If not, add a couple more occurrences to the list and repeat the 'going away' process.

Having selected the memory, you can put together a hoard of information surrounding it. Begin by jotting down your recollections, remembering that focussed, specific detail delivered in concrete terms is far more interesting than anything vague, abstract or general. Then concentrate on your senses, the root of the poem's imagery. If your memory fails you, ask yourself some questions about that time in your life rather than the specific event, such as *What did I like to wear? Where did we go on holiday? What was my favourite meal?* and so on. Sometimes these questions about the period rather than the event can rekindle the memories you're seeking.

Target event:

Recollections:

What could you see? (include physical surroundings, people, focal points, clothing):

What could you hear? (include natural and mechanical sounds and speech):

What could you smell? (ambient aromas, perfumes, food):

What could you taste? (allied with sense of smell):

What could you feel? (textures, temperature, wet or dry):

What emotional responses were evoked?

When these have been filled in, take another break for a few minutes and do something else. Come back to them and make any additions or alterations you think apt.

THE MESSAGE

What is your poem going to say to the reader? It may be as simple as *This happened to me and I'd like to share it* - or something more subtle, such as a comparison between then and now, an explanation of how a child's future is moulded by events in the teens, or an in-depth explanation of relationships.

Message:

Directly expressed or implied?

THE FIRST DRAFT

The content of the poem is delivered in stanzas of three lines with no rhyming or metrical requirements. The lines don't have to be of equal length. Each stanza should contain at least one concrete image. It makes life easier if you either narrate the event in chronological order or concentrate on one sense at a time, as in your original notes.

  Bear your message in mind, and make sure you are communicating it effectively, whether it's spelt out or implicit.

  As you draft the stanzas, be aware of the importance of correct sentence structuring, particularly with regard to main verbs, and punctuation.

  Any poem is enhanced by the addition of extra layers of meaning. Never forget the impact of added complexities.

Title:

Stanza 1

2

3

4

5

6

7

8

REVISION GUIDELINES

It's always a good idea to rest your draft before beginning the revision process. If you can allow yourself a week or two before looking at it again, you will have got over the excitement of completing the first draft and be able to view it with a more critical eye.

Start by asking yourself whether the poem is interesting to read, and whether it conveys its message effectively. Be prepared to start again if it fails on either of these points.

Check again that the technicalities of grammar and punctuation are applied correctly.

Look back at each stanza of the poem to see if every word it includes is the best - the perfect - word to communicate your thoughts. Be prepared to make changes:

- to use a different word that carries an added nuance of meaning or resonance.
- to change to a word that introduces an element of slant rhyme - similarity of sound - and so buttress the poetic 'feel' of the piece.
- to avoid repetition, unless it is part of the poem's dynamics.

Have another look at the order in which you have placed the stanzas. You may need to switch things around to be most effective.

Confirm that any additional layers to make the poem more complex don't make it wilfully obscure.

Allow your poem to settle again before working on any further revisions.

PROJECT TWO

Perhaps it's easier to write dark poetry about negative thoughts and reactions than upbeat material. This exercise is designed to produce a feel-good list poem including personal references, imaginative material and elements of humour.

PRE-WRITING

The key to this poem is clever use of lists, and so the initial notes take the form of a list. Start by deciding on the inclusion factor for your list. It could be something like *Reasons to Get out of Bed, Happiness Is ..., Good Things about Christmas* - anything about which you could find something positive to say. Include a number if you wish, eg. *Ten Days I'll Never Forget.*

List Heading:

Even if your heading/prospective title gives a number, aim for a longer list of elements - say 25. Go for the familiar responses everybody might have, and the obscure. Be serious and flippant. Be personal and detached. Be hackneyed and original. I've suggested a few thoughts to start you off:

- waking up to a sunny day
- knowing someone loves you
- the existence of the crunchie bar
- the knowledge that you'll never have to sit another exam - unless you want to

This exercise is another in which it helps to distance yourself from the writing for a bit, but here you can still think about it. Try to find some task that takes you away physically, but doesn't require great mental effort, such as walking the dog, gardening or ironing. While you are doing it, let your thoughts skim over other possibilities you could add to the list. Sometimes the best ideas come when you're away from the desk.

When you have amassed a good long list, attack it with coloured highlighters. Use one colour to mark all the ideas you want to include in the list poem, one for any idea you feel you could develop into a complete poem on its own, and a third if you find there's another strand of thought coming in which could create a further new poem.

While this 'three for the price of one' principle sounds good, it could be a little too convenient. There's always a danger of latching on to an idea, style, structure or form of wording and then using it over and over again. Yes, of course the ideas are there to be exploited, and of course you don't have to ditch them after a single use; just beware of turning a brilliant approach into your default device, and doing it to death.

THE MESSAGE

This needs to be nothing more than a simple *It made me feel good to write this - hope it makes you feel good to read it.* If you want to include anything more in-depth, you can.

Message:

THE FIRST DRAFT

Much of the work required by this poem has taken place in the pre-writing stage. You've already selected the ideas you want to include, and may have earmarked others for different poems to write later. Now you have two major challenges: putting them in the best order, and then establishing them as a poem rather than just a list.

Finding the order can be a study in randomness. Often the best list poems are those which ignore any logical progression of ideas and surprise the reader at every point. Sometimes the order is easy to establish, and you can simply jot down numbers alongside the relevant points. If the order doesn't present itself immediately, write your selected points on strips of paper and juggle them into different orders, seeing which works best.

When it comes to presenting the list as an actual poem, it's important to remember that moulding your piece into sentences will provide a narrative. Don't worry about incorporating rhyme and metre, but allow your list to flow in free verse. You could use a simple device of repetition, such as:

> It's waking up on a sunny day,
>
> knowing someone loves you;
>
> it's eating crunchie bars …

or with a phrase rather than a single word:

> You know it's a beautiful day
>
> when you wake up to sunshine
>
> and know someone loves you,
>
> eat crunchie bars for breakfast
>
> and realise you've passed your driving test.
>
> You know it's a beautiful day
>
> when …

Ideas could be introduced without the repeated word/s.

> Happiness is waking up to sunshine
>
> and knowing someone loves you.
>
> There is joy in chocolate bars,

> freedom in the knowing you'll never sit another exam.
>
> You can look around you and see ...

All these suggestions incorporate the list as a series of one-liners, but you may choose to say more about each experience:

> Your day starts with sunshine
>
> creeping through the crack of bedroom curtains,
>
> warming a blackbird's first song.
>
> You are loved, and your love
>
> reflects sun, basks in its own delight.
>
> You reach out, find the chocolate bar -
>
> a silly gift that fills you
>
> with its smooth coating,
>
> crams your mouth with sugar froth.

Producing a longer treatment in this way might indicate that your list needs adjusting. You may wish to jettison some of the points on it in the interests of tighter writing, or because they produce abstract rather than concrete images. (The example above demonstrates this in the woolly generalisation of lines 4/5.)

This treatment might need to be divided into separate stanzas, instead of appearing as a solid block of text. The stanzas do not have to be of equal length, but breaks are placed where the logic of the content suggests they should be.

Try developing your list as a poem on the page opposite, using the numbered spaces if you are presenting a simple list, and spanning two spaces per stanza if you are expanding on the points.

List heading/working title:

1st point

2nd

3rd

4th

5th

6th

7th

8th

9th

10th

REVISION GUIDELINES

A list started you off, so your first question to self should be: *Has this really become a poem, or is it still just a list?* Assuming that you're happy it's the former, begin your revision by checking through the list to see if each point on it does something for the reader. The 'something' may be to surprise, amuse, please, interest, inform, or maybe to elicit the response: *I've never thought of it like that.* If you read one of the points and find there's no impact, consider changing it for a different reference from your original set of ideas.

Read your poem aloud - a useful exercise for anything you write - and ask yourself whether it sounds poetic or pedestrian. Poetic does not, of course, mean littered with archaisms or full of wrenched syntax. It simply means that the way language has been used in taut and spare, with no wasted words, and that you have not resorted to a convoluted phrase when a single word would convey the same thing. The vocabulary should be contemporary, but should also reflect the beauty of word sounds and word combinations. You are speaking out in today's voice - but that voice is enriched and enhanced to form a poem.

One of the hardest things to assess is the feel-good factor that kick-started the poem. Probably the best way to reassure yourself about this is to read it through every couple of days for a fortnight, and see whether you feel elevated and delighted when you do so. If you do, it will cheer your day. If you don't ... back to the drawing board.

When you are happy with your poem, return to the original list where you used the highlighter pens, and explore the potential for poetry that remains undeveloped.

PROJECT THREE

Elizabethan sonnets have been around since … well, a few years before the first Elizabeth. They're enduringly popular, and can be written in today's English just as powerfully as they were in Shakespeare's language. These are the sonnets with the rhyme scheme: a b a b c d c d e f e f g g The lines are in iambic pentameter, with each of its five feet each consisting of an unstressed syllable followed by a stressed one.

PRE-WRITING

It's important to find a subject that will fit into the brevity and confines of a sonnet. You are going to have 140 syllables to play with in the fourteen lines, and all you have to do is to sparkle, be original, and enthral your readers. That's all.

    We'll use one of the most familiar themes for sonnets and write about an aspect of the natural world. This is a good area to explore as you can usually fit subject into form very happily. It's a bad area to explore as so many poets have been there before; so the need to find something new to say is paramount. After all, if you do nothing but rehash all the things other writers have said, you can't justify the time it takes a reader to study your poem. The reader's time is valuable; don't squander it.

    As the rhyme scheme indicates, Elizabethan sonnets break up neatly into three quatrains with alternate lines rhyming, and a final rhyming couplet. Traditionally there is a turn before the couplet, where the thrust of the poem changes and the final lines provide comment, a different point of view, something to make the reader think. We'll consider an additional mini-turn after each of the first two quatrains.

Think of something you have observed in a natural context - a sparrow on a twig, shells on the beach, poppies swaying in a field … whatever. Now decide what fascinates you about this, preferably an association that has never struck you before. For example, the sparrow could be twittering around like your infant school headmistress; how does the shell feel, redundant and vacated, with no future but being pounded down into sand? or how does the splash of red against green look from the air? Be imaginative. Be innovative.

Item seen:

Context:

Now let's consider extending the idea into a sonnet by jotting down a brief note for each part. This format presents you with a possible route, but play around with it to find the pattern that works best for your theme.

1st quatrain - content to describe the wider setting:

2nd quatrain - zooming in on the object of your observation:

3rd quatrain - further comment or additional thoughts about the object:

Final couplet - summing-up, fresh viewpoint, etc:

THE MESSAGE

This is usually encapsulated in that rhyming couplet at the end, but it helps to work towards it throughout the poem. It needs to be expressed briefly, and should reveal a truth, or prompt the reader to acknowledge *Yes, that's just how it is.*

Message:

THE FIRST DRAFT

For a sonnet to be successful, form and content should work in harmony to create a rich experience for the reader. So concentrate on rhyme and metre as well as the actual wording.

First quatrain - panorama:

1	a
2	b
3	a
4	b

Second quatrain - zooming in:

5	c
6	d
7	c
8	d

Third quatrain - additional:

9	e
10	f
11	e
12	f

Couplet - summing up/new angle:

13	g
14	g

REVISION GUIDELINES

We'll look first at the content of the poem. Check that detail and focus keep the picture sharp throughout the descriptive passage. Can you substitute a concrete word or phrase for an abstract or general one?

Is there a logical flow of ideas through the poem? Is there balance, with a fair distribution of content so that you are not devoting half the poem to one slight thought, and then rushing through quantities of material at breakneck speed? Is there a fresh approach after the turn, so that the final couplet holds the reader's interest and resonates in the memory? Is there anything new and original in the content to really grip the reader? If the answer to this question is *no,* be sure to put it right before you finalise the poem ready for submission.

Now look at the form. Have your fourteen lines followed the rhyme scheme indicated? Are the rhymes natural and unforced? Have you been able to keep to the rhyme scheme without prejudicing grammar and syntax?

Are all the lines iambic pentameter, starting with an unstressed syllable and then alternating these with stressed syllables until there are ten syllables in all? If you have deviated from the strict pattern of stresses, is it to form one of the standard variants? The main ones are reversing the first foot of the line to create a trochee, with a stressed syllable followed by an unstressed, then returning to iambic feet; and the feminine ending, an extra unstressed syllable added to the end of the line.

Throughout the revision, see if you can come up with a title which is specific - and interesting enough to tempt the browser to stop and read.

PROJECT FOUR

Supernatural phenomena have fuelled writers' output for centuries, and the good news is that this source of ideas is bottomless. The only boundaries are the limits of your own imagination. You can take and adapt any supernatural story you know, or invent a new one. For the purposes of this poem, we'll demonstrate the idea of ascribing power to an 'ordinary' object.

PRE-WRITING

Begin by selecting the object and its unexpected ability. It could be a teaspoon that initiates time travel into the past or future; a key that can open any lock; an umbrella that makes you invisible. Let your imagination go, and don't deny the child in you, whose thinking will be freer than yours.

Object:

Power:

     Now decide who will use the object - yourself, another person you've created, or a character from history or literature.

User:

     Next, you need to think about the narrative. This may start with a difficult emotional position your character is in; or they may be in physical peril, and the object's power removes the danger or transports them to a safe place; or the character's deepest desires are fulfilled; or the object is malevolent and brings evil. Other people may be involved, or the character may be alone. Again, let your imagination run free.

Narrative:

The final stage of this poem is the denouement, where the situation is resolved - happily or unhappily - and the future of the magical object is determined. Alternatively, you could end on a note of uncertainty.

Denouement:

Object's future:

Before you move on from the pre-writing part of the exercise, ask yourself two questions:
- ᐊ do I believe in this product of my imagination? If you can't suspend your own disbelief, a reader is unlikely to be able to.
- ᐊ will this fit into the form of a poem? You may have an embryo short story or even novel on your hands.

THE MESSAGE

A great deal of fantasy material is written purely for entertainment. That's fine - but you do have an opportunity to include a message. Maybe your powerful object is a metaphor for a different phenomenon, or there's a truth to be conveyed, such as *be careful of what you wish for.*

Message:

THE FIRST DRAFT

Although it may be tempting to launch into the poem following the pattern of the pre-writing notes, you might prefer to begin in the thick of the action. Think of a gripping way to establish character and problem in an opening free verse stanza. Write in the present tense to make it seem more immediate, using stanza breaks to give readers a chance to draw breath. Then allow the narrative to carry the action forward to a climax before the denouement and aftermath.

Possible title:

Action/establishing situation:

Narrative:

Climax:

Denouement:

Aftermath:

REVISION GUIDELINES

Following the hint that started the first draft, ask yourself whether this poem begins and ends in the right place. Is there the right amount of explanation, too much or too little?

While you are engaged in reading the poem, is the account convincing? Do you want to know more about the situation? Are you compelled to read the poem to the end?

Given that a fantasy situation makes its own rules, have you kept to these rules? If the object/power is a pencil that can write down the correct answer to any question, don't let it suddenly start making a cup of tea or spinning the earth faster.

Whether you followed the suggestion to use present tense or chose to write in the past, have you kept to the same tense throughout?

Look at the lineation of your poem. As it's in free verse, there is no line end indicator. Check that you haven't split phrases in a clumsy way, or left a weak word at a line's end, its strongest point. It's better to place a more significant word there to allow it to benefit from the hint of extra emphasis the line's end offers.

Consider the wording. Could you introduce any more elements of slant rhyme, particularly assonance, alliteration and consonance? For example, if you took the phrase *a night filled with dreams* you could introduce these by changing it to:

- sl*ee*p filled with dr*ea*ms (assonance)
- night of *d*eep *d*reams (alliteration)
- night's cal*m* drea*m* (consonance)
- *s*wam*p s*lee*p* with dreams (full consonance)

PROJECT FIVE

Have you ever used your newspaper as a source of ideas for poems? The beauty of it is that a new source is generated every day. Any part of the paper can trigger a poem. For this exercise we'll concentrate on a human interest news item. There is just one caveat: trading on other people's problems may seem distasteful. Use your own sensitivity and good manners to know what to copy detail by detail - and what to change beyond recognition.

PRE-WRITING

This begins with thorough reading. You can ignore the big stories, the political and world events, and the celebs behaving badly. Instead, study all the news items that are about ordinary people and the events that change their lives for better or worse. When you have read them all, put the paper aside for a few minutes and see which remains most strongly in your memory. This is your target story. If you have a good recollection of more than one, choose the account that makes you laugh or makes you shudder. It has better potential for evoking emotions in the reader.

Target story:

Identify three characters/objects from the report. For example, in a tale about someone's dog producing fifteen pups, you might have the dog owner, the proud Mum-of-fifteen, and the ball that isn't being taken to the park as its owner is too busy puppyminding.

Character/object one:

Character/object two:

Character/object three:

    Now write a maximum of 100 words in prose from the angle of each of these, giving their side of the story.

Character/object one viewpoint:

Character/object two viewpoint:

Character/object three viewpoint:

Which was the easiest to write? Which produces the most interesting account? At this stage, select the person or object who will be at the heart of your poem. From now, you will see what goes on through the eyes and thinking of your choice. Be prepared to write in the first person. (You may decide to change to third person at a later stage, but start by using *I*).

Look again at the newspaper story, considering the point made in the introduction to this project. Would you feel comfortable about narrating the account as it happened? Think around the situation. How could you give it a different spin to enhance the poem? Choose a few scenarios that might be worth pursuing:

The next task is to feed in an additional factor. If your writing is to fascinate the reader, it needs to include something extra to elevate it from enhanced account to enriched poem. Also, linking in any extra element gives you more hope of writing an original poem, as there's less chance of another poet matching both your trains of thought. The factor could be another strand of narrative or backstory, emotional input, or a separate random element of your choice.

Additional factor:

Think how you will end the account. Can you enthral your readers, and leave them with food for thought?

Ending:

THE MESSAGE

The obvious message is just *look what happened and how it changed things*. You might also consider communicating an emotional message by enticing readers into the deepest depths of the story.

Message:

THE FIRST DRAFT

Think carefully about how you will launch into the account and establish your character identity. Remember the maxim *show, don't tell* and avoid over-explaining. The poem may be in any style, free verse, blank verse or a traditional form, and presented as a single block or broken down into stanzas.

Title:

First person narrative:

Keep the newspaper cutting alongside the draft.

REVISION GUIDELINES

Start the revision process by reading the first draft silently and then aloud. Now do the same with the cutting that prompted it. Ask yourself these questions:

- Is the poem more interesting than the report, or vice versa? (The poem should win!)
- Is my chosen voice appropriate and true?
- Have I managed to put more into the poem than the story itself has to say?
- Will a reader take something more away from studying the poem than from reading the report?

If you are happy with the answers, proceed to the next stage and look at the form and structuring of the poem. Did you select the perfect vehicle to communicate your ideas? Would it have been better with rhyme, in a different tense, or in another person? Are sentence construction, punctuation and grammar adding to the effectiveness of the poem, or detracting from it?

Look again at the content. Does it include everything you want to say? Do you need anything more? Have you overstated or expressed the obvious?

End each revision with the two huge questions:

- Would I be embarrassed to have the protagonists of the news story read my poem?
- Would I be proud or ashamed to see this poem in a book or magazine with my name beside it?

PROJECT SIX

Sometimes a word picked at random can be the starting point for a brilliant poem. The joy of it is that you approach the blank sheet of paper without an inkling of the poem that is to come, and have the opportunity to flex your poetic muscles on a theme you might never have considered covering.

PRE-WRITING

Select your random word by sticking a pin in a page, or switching on the TV or radio and taking the first word you hear. Now use that word to trigger an exercise in flow writing. Allow yourself a fixed period of time, such as three minutes, and set an alarm to go off after that time. Starting from the word you picked, write down all the thoughts that come into your head spontaneously. Don't strain after a logical flow of ideas, just keep writing without taking your pen from the paper. Don't stop writing. If you suddenly find you're stuck, repeat the last word over and over again until it sparks a new thought. Don't look back at what you have written. Wait until the timer sounds.

Starting word:

When the allotted time has passed, read through your work. Again, don't worry about any thread of logic, but instead look to see what you have written that fascinates you, prompts you to recall a half-forgotten memory, or puzzles you. Underline three words or phrases you find interesting. Any one of them, or a combination of two or three, may kickstart an idea for a poem. If that happens, use the space below to jot down some notes. If it does not, take one of your words/phrases and and use it to start a repeat of the flow writing exercise, following the same instructions.

Notes/second flow write:

You can repeat this process as often as required.

When you have selected the idea that is worth exploring, your next task is to decide where it's going and how it will work as a poem. What type of poem are you prompted to write? It could be descriptive, narrative, emotional, humorous, philosophical .. the nature of your idea will dictate.

Type:

How do you envisage the emerging poem? Will there be rhyme and/or metre? Will it take a set form, or use free verse? How will it be laid out on the page?

Pattern:

What poetic devices will you be using to bring the poem to life? Will there be clever metaphors, vivid images, unexpected vocabulary?

Devices:

Because there is such an open brief for this project, it would be a good idea to work a few lines in a number of different styles in order to see which seems most effective.

1st style:

2nd style:

3rd style:

4th style:

THE MESSAGE

The special information you want to convey to your reader may be in the flow writing, choice of words, or second flow/notes. Jot it down now, or after you've completed the first draft.

Message:

THE FIRST DRAFT

Decide which style of writing seems best for your poem - remembering that there will be plenty of time to change it during the redrafting and revision process.

Bear in mind that a poem with the ability to surprise you, its creator, will have the best potential for surprising the reader.

In the spirit of the trigger for this poem, see if you can get words onto paper swiftly and without becoming too bogged down on any part of it. Again, remind yourself about that opportunity to re-work it later.

Title:

REVISION GUIDELINES

Because of the way the poem began, the first point of revision is to ask yourself that vital question, *Does this piece have anything to say?* If it does, and if it is being said in a persuasive manner, be reassured. If it doesn't, eat a large cream cake, go back to your original notes, and start again.

When it comes to checking the invidual words and phrases you have used in the poem, see if there's anything you can cut - or rather, prune, which is a more creative and empowering task.

Look first to see if you have repeated yourself, either by using a word or variant on it twice in close proximity (other than repetition for artistic reasons) or by communicating the same message in two different ways. For example, you could *look up at the sky* but as the nature of *sky* makes the *up* redundant, *up* could be cut. Sometimes a passage in the poem, maybe a whole stanza, is summed up in the lines that follow, and therefore its message is reiterated unnecessarily.

We all have favourite words and phrases that crop up over and over again. Watch out for these, too, and keep a rein on them.

One tiny word that can often be dropped and makes your poem seem instantly tighter is the definite article. *The* is used all the time in speech and in prose writing, and can seldom be dispensed with. In a poem, however, you can lose every non-essential *the* and give your writing a tauter, more poetic 'feel'.

PROJECT SEVEN

Is there artistic talent buzzing away inside you? If there isn't, don't worry. This exercise involves drawing, but you are the only person who will see it. It starts with a very simple idea, and then adds more complexity as it builds up into a poem.

PRE-WRITING

Think of a room in your home - but not the one you're in now. Sketch it in the space below. It's better if you can add colour. Your sketch should be as detailed as you can make it, and should include furniture, pictures, ornaments, etc.

Now take your sketch into the room you've drawn. Compare it with the actual room. Is there anything you've omitted? Have you included something that isn't there, and if so, what? Does the perspective work, or is your picture out of proportion with a giant chair or tiny window? Is the picture more accurate than you could have imagined?

Make a note of the feature, the discrepancy - or surprising accuracy - that interests you the most.

Feature:

What is its significance?

This will be the focus of the poem, but it needs to be clothed in additional material to create the actual piece. The story may be close to your life and to your target room, or you can use all your imaginative resources. Extend your thinking to encompass new possibilities, domestic occurrences, fears and other emotions, characters who have visited, or 'friends' who have not. Let your imagination run wild as you create a narrative. Start with observations that interest you:

When the route into a poem begins to suggest itself to you, create a list of soundbites. These are little fragments of poems, descriptions, thoughts and ideas that may become part of the poem or may eventually be jettisoned. Don't worry about putting them in order - just get them down.

Soundbite 1

Soundbite 2

Soundbite 3

Soundbite 4

Soundbite 5

Soundbite 6

Can you feel any rush of ideas? Play with the soundbites, changing their order, building on them, writing the opposite message in response to them, exploring them in different wordings, trying out rhyme in them. Refer back to the initial drawing if it seems helpful.

Stay at the note phase until you can feel those ideas swelling and building up, needing to be released. If there's insufficient pressure, go away and do something else but still let your mind play with the soundbites. When the pressure's insisting, pour out a torrent of poetry to form your first draft.

THE MESSAGE

You are examining the way mind and memory can play tiny tricks on you. It can be an edgy, disconcerting experience. If you wish, you can communicate that edginess, a hint of uncertainty, in your poem.

Message:

THE FIRST DRAFT

Don't be too concerned with the final form of the poem. You may find it helps to use some of those original soundbites, or variations of them. If you wish, link them together by means of a repeated phrase designed to unsettle, something like *It wasn't there* or *Nobody noticed* perhaps, which should appear at the start or end of each stanza at this point, but may be cut in revision.

Draft in rhyme or free verse, choosing your vocabulary for its precision of meaning and also for the sounds your words produce when the piece is spoken aloud.

Title:

Text possibly incorporating link:

REVISION GUIDELINES

Start the revision by looking at the drawing once again, and recalling making comparisons between it and the actual room. Look at the poem as a whole, checking whether you have achieved what you originally set out to do through your writing. If you did, that's fine. If you didn't, that's fine too. As long as the end result is a poem, the exercise has worked.

That moment's review of your work is just for you to see how the initial sketch turned into a poem, and for your own interest. The next stage is the reader's interest. Tick off each of these points as you confirm them:

1. Is there a constant movement forward through the content of the poem, or does it stall or go around in circles?
2. Are images used throughout the poem, so that it appeals to the senses of the reader?
3. Is the wording chosen with care?
4. Do rhyme and metre, if used, appear natural and unforced?
5. Are your sentences logical and grammatical?
6. Is the title enticing?

PROJECT EIGHT

Rhyming couplets are incredibly difficult to do well, and while they are fun to use in comic poems, they can sound trite and trivialise more serious subjects unless handled with great care. The trick with this poem is to use the rhymed couplet in lines of widely varied lengths, rather than in uniform, metrical lines, in order to communicate lighthearted anecdotal material.

PRE-WRITING

The best writers learn to capitalise on other people's stories, so although this form can be used with virtually any content, we'll experiment with a 'second hand' tale. To pick the story, think back to the last time you were in relaxed company. Who told a tale that made you laugh? Can you remember the details of it, or at least enough to supply a skeleton of an idea that you can flesh out from your own imagination? If you can't recall a story, chat with a friend and ask what they've seen or done recently that raised a laugh.

Story in brief prose summary:

The narrative of the tale will give you an order of events which you can follow. It's good to have a lighter poem start with a bang and end with a punchline. If a brilliant idea for these strikes you at any time during the pre-writing and first draft, jot it down before you risk forgetting it.

Start:

Punchline:

You can add to the light note by including witty rhymes. Have fun playing with language and seeking out some good rhymes for vocabulary that relates to the story, eg.

- disaster   in plaster
- Friday   pie day
- toast   ghost

Compile your own list, knowing that you may not use all the rhymes you select.

Now experiment with the different line lengths, remembering that if the lines are almost the same length, variants will sound like mistakes. If they differ considerably, the form will be recognised at once. Don't worry about the context for the moment - just explore the pattern, eg.

    They came to see

    whatever could have happened to me

    when I tripped, stumbled and fell down the ladder.

    I was madder

    than anybody could ever guess

    and frankly the rest of my life was in a bit of a mess …

Try a few general lines on any subject:

Next try a fragment from your story in the same form:

THE MESSAGE

Is this just for amusement, or is there something deeper that you are intending to communicate?

Message:

THE FIRST DRAFT

When you feel you have got under the skin of the form, it's time to begin writing the actual poem. You are simply going to narrate an account of events in chronological order, remembering all the time to keep to wildly varied line lengths. It's surprising how easy it is to default to similar line lengths when you are immersed in the tale.

  This form seems to look best on the page when you write it in one chunk rather than in seperate stanzas.

  The beauty of the random line lengths is that you are never in a position where you might risk compromising syntax or forcing the text in order to place rhymes, so the poem will read naturally.

  Remember to keep the writing light and use a conversational approach. The chiming sound of the rhyming couplets will ensure that the essence of poetry does not get lost in the tone of your chatty 'voice'.

  This form of poetry lends itself to the spoken word, so keep speaking it aloud throughout the production of the first draft as well as when you reach the revision stage.

Title:

REVISION GUIDELINES

Find a sympathetic friend who will read the poem out to you and allow you to hear the words rather than read them for yourself. Listen for three major factors:

- Is it a good tale well told?
- Does the anecdote have a conversational tone?
- Does the rhyming work?

When you are reassured on these points from the listener's angle, begin your study of the ms.

Check that you have used interesting rhymes rather than resorting to the predictable *moon/June* school of rhyming. Given the poem's structure, you may feel it is best to keep to full rather than slant rhymes, but if you have included any slant rhymes, make sure they are very close in sound. *Moon/tomb* would work a lot better than *moon/most*.

Look carefully at the beginning and ending of the poem. Have you over-explained in setting up or concluding the story? Allow the reader's intelligence the opportunity to work alongside your words.

PROJECT NINE

Nothing grisly here, but the next poem is inspired by body parts. These are a good source of ideas. Apart from the physical form, they are used in metaphor and idiom, and many of the terms for them are homonyms, eg. *foot* is a measure.

PRE-WRITING

The preparation for this poem takes the form of a spider diagram - also known as a brainstorming or mindmapping technique if you want to annoy the PC police. The next page has a single word in the middle. This is at the centre of the poem. Every idea allied to it, from physical description to sayings, similes, personal references, idioms, other meanings, facts and factoids, tradition and mythology, should appear on the page. Each fresh angle of connection is indicated by a spoke radiating outwards from the central word. Allied connections branch out from the primary ones. A couple of connections have been written in to illustrate this.

When the page is covered with references, study it carefully. Does anything surprise you? Are there any links to one connection that also relate to another? Get out the highlighter pens again to group series of words and phrases.

Keep your poem radar functioning while you are doing this, and be alert to every possibility that might be worth exploration. Don't throw your spider diagram away when you've written one poem. There could be more to come.

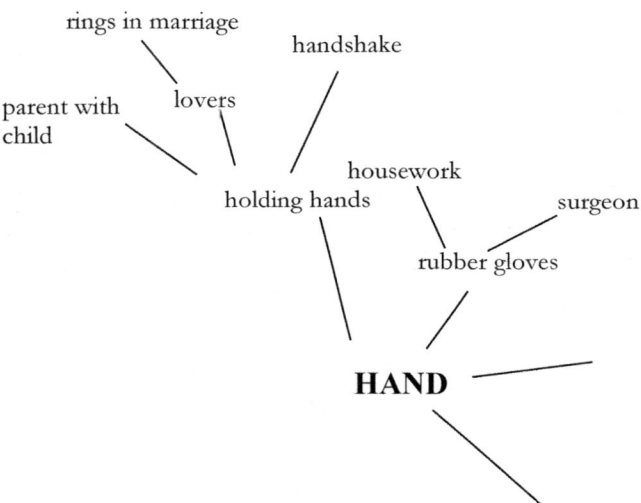

Much of the transition from pre-writing to first draft for this exercise takes place in the head. Think about your diagram, play with some of the ideas there, and never lose sight of the fact that you are looking for a poem. If an idea presents itself, no problem. If it doesn't, take whichever aspect of the theme you wish to follow and do some research. If, say, you were interested in fingerprints, you could learn something of their history and importance. If you wanted to consider the washing of hands, you might research sayings such as *wash your hands of* something, practices that involve ritual handwashing, or the way a doctor would scrub up for an operation. When you feel that you yourself are intrigued by any aspect of the theme, it's time to launch into the first draft.

THE MESSAGE

This will depend entirely on the connections you've selected. Message:

THE FIRST DRAFT

There is no set route to follow: you are mapping the journey for yourself while you travel through the unknown territory of your ideas. Let your pen roam freely, and be vigilant in case pen, head or heart starts to channel the poem into an exciting new direction. Only make sure that the form in which your poem emerges is adhered to throughout the draft, so that there is technical harmony in the dynamics of the poem.

Title:

REVISION GUIDELINES

Offer yourself a list of opposing possibilities, and decide - truthfully - which apply to your poem. Go through the whole list before you start making any alterations, marking the areas that need attention.

- series of notes or realised poem?
- true poem or result of an exercise? (Can be both!)
- fluent or disjointed?
- structured or partly-formed sentences?
- convincing rhymes if used, or weak, familiar rhymes?
- little sound similarity or plenty of slant rhyme if free verse?
- plain or heightened vocabulary?
- clinical or atmospheric?
- original or heard-it-all-before?
- dull and pedestrian or vibrant with colour?
- title uninspiring or tempting the reader in?
- rich or poor in literary devices?
- states the obvious or opens new windows in the mind?
- tautly written or over-wordy?
- starting and ending at interesting points or banal?

PROJECT TEN

Write the week. We'll look at a structured poem or sequence of poems following the days of the week. The final version may mention each day, or the day names can be omitted. This type of diary poem can be written on any subject. We'll be very British, and focus on the weather.

PRE-WRITING

Start by choosing your weather condition, which may be expected or surprising, ordinary or dramatic.

Weather: Make a list of words and phrases connected with your chosen weather conditions. Try to be original - poets have been describing sun, rain and snow for centuries:

Remember the value of introducing a second focus point to give you more to say and an increased chance of being original in your writing. This extra factor could be the narrative of a series of events, or simply another device to animate the poem.

Extra factor:

Location is tied in with climate. Think about where you want the poem to take place, and whether this same location would work alongside your extra factor.

Location:

When you have gathered some ideas for the poem, you will need to divide it into seven chunks of material. These could be quite lengthy - if you have decided to produce a sequence, there could be a whole poem for each day - or extremely brief. For example, using rain in each case:

MONDAY MOURNING - weather coupled with a death

1   Monday: It rained

as I sat beside your hospital bed,

… 2nd person character dies ...

2   Tuesday: Rain drummed on the roof

as I held the telephone,

… info. about telling people what happened ...

3   Wednesday: It poured with rain …

… funeral arrangements …   etc. each to be a stanza

and briefly:

BLACKPOOL HOLIDAY - weather coupled with a holiday

1   Saturday: we arrived. It rained.
2   Sunday: went to the beach. It rained.
3   Monday: went up the tower. It rained.
4   Tuesday: … activity … rain …
5   Wednesday … activity …   etc. each to be one line

You get the idea? Try dividing up your content in this way, including both weather condition and extra factor.

Incidentally, you will see from both the examples that the title is an essential part of scene-setting. Think carefully about this as it will affect the whole of the poem.

Title:

Day 1:

Day 2:

Day 3:

Day 4:

Day 5:

Day 6:

Day 7:

When you have had some thoughts about the content of each day, decide where to start your week. As the examples demonstrate, it could be on any day.

THE MESSAGE

You might want to communicate something about the events that can change a life more quickly than the weather changes, share images about a spectacular landscape in certain conditions, or look at the impact of weather on people and places.

Message:

THE FIRST DRAFT

Writing in any form of rhymed patterns with or without metre, or free verse supported by slant rhyme, develop your notes for the seven days.

If you are producing a single poem to cover the whole week, make sure that your individual days fit together as part of a realised piece. If your imagination takes flight and you want to write a complete poem for each day, you can create them all in the same pattern, or use a range of different forms.

This style of poem offers a good opportunity for you to add extra layers to give more meaning and depth.

NB If you are writing a lengthy poem for each day, draft the first day only on this sheet, ignoring the stanza breaks.

Title:

Day 1: (state the day of the week for each stanza)

Day 2:

Day 3:

Day 4:

Day 5:

Day 6:

Day 7:

Concluding stanza if required:

REVISION GUIDELINES

Don't forget that although the day-by-day device kick-started this poem, referring to each day by name is an option, not a requirement. What works best for the piece you're developing?

Ask yourself how many layers of meaning have been threaded through the poem. Are you happy with them? Do they feel natural, or synthetic and grafted on?

Have you managed to make the weather references sound fresh and original?

Does the poem come to life on the page? Does it work when read aloud?

Look at every single word in the poem one at a time. Is it the perfect choice for that context? Could you substitute any of the words for ones that carry extra resonances?

What are you planning to do with the poem when it's finished? Will you use it in readings, enter it for a competition, submit it to a magazine, or keep it in the drawer?

Do you like the poem? Giving an honest answer doesn't alter its effectiveness, but it offers an insight into your engagement with your own writing.

PROJECTS REVISITED

When you have worked through all the projects, here's another idea for each source to start a new poem.
1. Write about a more recent memory, using tercets or quatrain stanzas.
2. Create a list poem of things that make you angry, bored, terrified, etc.
3. Write a sonnet rooted in an emotion rather than an object/landscape, still using concrete terms and imagery.
4. Take a supernatural creature, such as a ghost, vampire or unicorn, and have it materialise unexpectedly in the 'real world'. Follow the same route of establishment, narrative, denouement and aftermath.
5. Focus on one of the newspaper's regular features, such as the horoscope page, sports reviews or TV listings.
6. Pick five words at random. Write a meaningful poem in any form that includes them all - and makes sense.
7. Get a holiday/art picture postcard. Study it carefully for a few minutes, then turn it over and create your own sketch of the picture. Compare your version with the original, and create a poem from the discrepancies.
8. Using the same form, write a poem describing a special holiday or a memory from the early days of childhood.
9. Repeat the idea using a different body part.
10. Using the months of the year instead of days of the week, write a poem about the course of a relationship.

ANOTHER TEN POEMS

Try these ideas for poems, remembering the all-important stages of pre-writing, first draft and revision.

1. Read to write. Study a literary magazine and use a poem you enjoy as a template for your next piece. Emulate its pattern and route, but use original content.
2. Write a poem based on all aspects of a colour.
3. Go to a museum and write about one of the artefacts.
4. Focus on a game, choosing from a card, board or playground game. Write about playing it, or use the imagery and jargon from it to deliver your message.
5. Write about an iconic pair of shoes - Cinderella's glass slipper, the latest must-have trainers, Nureyev's dance shoes, 1966 football boots. Let the shoes narrate.
6. Write a sequence of poems about a wedding or other celebration, focussing on the range of characters there.
7. Write a poem in the form of a letter to someone you know or a celebrity, living or dead, communicating an important message to them.
8. Do you have a little possession - a trinket of no intrinsic value - that means a lot to you? Write about its significance, and give it some additional resonance.
9. Remember any dream or nightmare you have had. Write a narrative poem as if you were living through it.
10. Write a poem about a favourite holiday - or the holiday from hell.

Printed in Dunstable, United Kingdom

76511941R00047